North Carolina Fish Species

Game Fish & Panfish

Billy Grinslott – Kinsey Marie Books

ISBN - 9781968228446

Redear sunfish are known for their red or orange-edged gill flaps. They are a type of sunfish that thrive in warm, quiet waters, feeding primarily on mollusks and snails, and can grow up to 12 inches and weigh as much as 2 pounds. They are also known as shellcracker, due to their diet and the way they crush shells. The redear sunfish will thrive in most warm-water lakes and streams.

Spotted sunfish are commonly found in backwater streams, coastal plain rivers, and ponds. They are known for their iridescent blue eye patch and small size. They are often called stumpknockers, because they love to hang out in and feed around submerged logs, stumps, and other woody debris. They thrive in warmer, slow-moving waters with sandy or rocky bottoms, and biting well on lures and bait.

The Flier is a small, sunfish known for its olive-green color, rows of dark spots, and a dark teardrop or streak below its eye, with large dorsal and anal fins. It inhabits slow-moving, clear waters in the Southern U.S. coastal plains and Mississippi river basin. They feed on insects, snails, worms, leeches, crustaceans, and small fish, also some phytoplankton.

Dollar sunfish are pint-sized sunfish, typically reaching 4-5 inches in length. They have a black opercular flap, the flap covering the gills, that is adorned with wavy blue lines or specks. They inhabit pools of creeks and small to medium rivers, as well as swamps and areas with cover like woody debris.

The bluegill also considered a sunfish is the most popular fish to fish for. They are called pan fish because they are about the size of a frying pan. Bluegills love to eat insects and bugs. They have good vision and rely on their keen eyesight to feed. Three types in this group are the Bluegill, Sunfish, and Pumpkinseed.

The Redbreast sunfish has a red-yellow chest and belly with rusty brown spots on their body. The species is known for its distinctive grunting vocalizations, which are produced by grinding their teeth together. Redbreast sunfish can survive in oxygen-poor environments by using their gills to extract oxygen from air bubbles trapped in aquatic vegetation.

The Blue spotted sunfish is a small freshwater fish known for its vibrant blue spots and tolerance for acidic low oxygen waters. They are native to the southeastern and eastern United States, inhabiting ponds, rivers, and backwaters with dense vegetation. They are one of the smallest fish in their family, typically reaching a maximum length of about 3.7 inches. Both males and females have light blue or white spots, but males tend to have more intense and vibrant spotting. They have a relatively short lifespan, typically living around 5 years.

The Green Sunfish is blue green in color. It has yellow flecks on both its scales and some parts of its sides. The Green Sunfish also has broken blue stripes which is why some people confuse it with the Bluegill. Green Sunfish are very adaptable. They can live in any body of water that has vegetation or weeds. Green sunfish are opportunistic feeders, consuming insects, small fish, and other invertebrates.

Banded Sunfish got their name because they have darker lines that run vertically on their sides. They also have a rounded tail with spots on their body, tail and fins. Banded sunfish are typically only about 2 inches long, making them one of the smallest sunfish. Their small size makes them vulnerable to larger fish, so they thrive in protected areas. Banded sunfish prefer slow-moving, vegetated waters like swamps, ponds, and backwaters of creeks

The Pumpkinseed is also known as pond perch, sun perch, and punky's sunfish. It can be found in numerous lakes, ponds, and rivers. It is their body shape resembling the seed of a pumpkin, that inspired their name. Pumpkinseed sunfish have speckles on their orangish colored sides and back, with a yellow to orange belly and chest. They are active during the day and rest at night near the bottom or in shelter areas.

The Mud Sunfish is a secretive, small freshwater fish known for its stocky body, large mouth, and distinctive dark stripes. It prefers to live in slow-moving, tannin-stained waters like swamps, bogs, ponds, and backwaters with soft, silty bottoms and aquatic plants. Their color ranges from olive to brownish tan. They are usually small, rarely exceeding 6 to 8 inches in length.

A Roanoke bass is a rare, native sunfish, related to rock bass. It's known for its dark olive-green color or smaller spots. It prefers to live in clean, flowing water in creeks and small rivers with rocky bottoms but is sensitive to siltation. While similar to the common rock bass, Roanoke bass have fewer, smaller spots and scaleless cheeks, along with a slightly concave forehead, making them distinct.

The Rock Bass is not actually a bass but a member of the sunfish family. They are often called red eye or goggle eye due to their distinctive bright red eyes. The biggest Rock Bass ever caught on record weighs about three pounds and was a little over one foot long. Rock bass prefer waters with rocky vegetated areas, that's how they got their name.

The Warmouth is a member of the Rock Bass, Green Sunfish and Bluegill family. They can survive in low oxygen environments while other fish cannot. Warmouth can thrive in muddy water, when other fish can't. Warmouth are often confused with rock bass. The difference between the two is in the anal fin. Warmouth have three spines on the anal fin ray and rock bass have six spines.

The two most famous perches are the common perch and the yellow perch. The yellow perch has a brilliant greenish yellow color with orange fins. The yellow perch is the biggest one and can grow to a size of 18 inches. It's also known as the jumbo perch. The other type of perch is the white perch. The biggest Yellow Perch caught in North Carolina weighed 2 pounds, 9 ounces.

White perch grow seven to ten inches in length and rarely weigh more than one pound. They have a silvery body with faint lines on the sides. The white perch is an opportunistic feeder. Young feed primarily on zooplankton and adults feed on aquatic insect larvae, minnows and fish eggs. White Perch is a euryhaline species, inhabiting fresh, brackish and coastal waters. The biggest White Perch caught in North Carolina weighed 2 pounds, 0.8 ounces.

There are two main types of crappies. The white crappie and the black crappie. They are also members of the sunfish family. The difference between the white and black crappie is one has dark spots and the other has dark lines and is lighter in color. The white crappie has six dorsal fin spines, whereas the black crappie has eight dorsal fin spines. The white crappie can grow bigger and more of the bigger white crappie are caught in North America. The North Carolina state record for Black Crappie is 4 lbs. 15 oz.

Bowfins can breathe both air and water, putting them at an advantage in low-oxygen waters. Bowfins are often described as prehistoric relics. This is because species can be traced to fossils from the Cretaceous, Eocene and Jurassic period. The biggest officially recognized Bowfin in North Carolina weighed 17 lbs. 15 oz.

There are few different species of Gar, the Longnose gar, Short nose and Alligator gar. The Long Nose Gar got its name because of its long mouth that looks like an alligator's mouth. The alligator gar is one of the biggest freshwater fish growing up to 10 feet long. The world record for a catch was set at 327 pounds. The biggest documented gar caught in North Carolina is a longnose gar weighing 19 pounds, 10.5 ounces.

Redhorse are large, bottom-feeding freshwater sucker fish known for their reddish fins, and molar-like throat teeth that they use to crush mollusks. They inhabit in clear rivers with gravelly bottoms, where they feed on insects and detritus. They spawn in spring, often migrating upstream. They are popular with anglers for their strong fight, when catching them in swift currents. They can grow to around 18 pounds and 30 inches long.

Carp have long been an important food fish to humans. Carp are bottom feeders for the most part and their mouth is made like a suction cup, so they can suck food off the bottom. Carp are good for a lake because they help clean the bottom of the lake. Carp are introduced for aquatic vegetation control and can grow very large. The biggest carp officially recorded in North Carolina is a Grass Carp weighing 68 lbs., 12 oz.

The black, brown and yellow bullhead are part of the catfish family. They usually only grow to about 10 inches long. They use their whiskers to help find food. The bullhead is the most common member of the catfish family. Bullheads live in the water containing low oxygen levels. They can survive on low oxygen areas, where other fish can't. The biggest bullhead caught in North Carolina is a 4-pound Brown Bullhead.

White catfish are interesting because they are smaller than other common catfish species like channel catfish, they have a wider head and lack the black spots of channel catfish. White catfish are the smallest of the large North American catfish species. The White catfish has white chin barbells, which distinguish it from other species. There are four pairs of barbels, whiskers around the mouth, two on the chin, one at the angle of the mouth, and one behind the nostril. The biggest White Catfish caught in North Carolina weighed 13 pounds.

Flathead Catfish, their body is wide but flattened and very low in height. Both eyes are on the top of the flattened head, giving excellent vision to see upward. Flathead catfish live mainly in large bodies of water like big rivers and reservoirs. They prefer deep pools of water. The biggest Flathead Catfish caught in North Carolina, and the current state record, is 78 pounds, 14 ounces.

The Channel Catfish are the most fished catfish species with around 8 million anglers fishing for them per year. Channel catfish have taste buds all over their body, making them highly sensitive to the taste and smell of food. They also have barbels (whiskers) around their mouths, which are used for sensing and tasting food. They use sound waves to communicate with each other. They can also produce alarm substances to warn other catfish of danger. The biggest Channel Catfish caught in North Carolina, and the current state record, is 27 pounds, 7 ounces.

Blue catfish are known for their size, reaching over 100 pounds. Blue catfish, like other catfish, lack scales and have smooth skin. They have barbels (whiskers) around their mouths, which are used for sensing and tasting food. They are generally slate blue on the back and silvery/white on the underside. The biggest blue catfish caught in North Carolina, and the current state record, weighed 127.1 pounds.

White Bass or striped bass range in color from a silvery white to a pale green. Their backs are mostly black, while their sides and belly are pale with stripes running along them. White Bass are related to Striped Bass and sometimes called wipers. The general world record for a white bass is around 6.8 pounds.

The Bodie Bass is a popular nickname for the Hybrid Striped Bass, a cross between a male White Bass and a female Striped Bass, known for its broken stripes, deep body, and excellent fighting ability. It's a favorite game fish in many freshwater reservoirs, prized for its aggressive nature, often caught with spoons, jigs, or live bait, especially in cooler months. They are sterile and do not reproduce naturally, so they are stocked in lakes and rivers by state hatcheries. They can grow to significant sizes, often reaching several pounds within three years. The biggest Bodie Bass officially recorded in North Carolina weighed 17 lbs, 7 oz.

Striped bass are often called Stripers. Striped bass live in both salt and fresh water. Striped bass have very sensitive eyes and will seek deep water when the sun is out. Striped bass have a preferred water temperature range of from 55° F to 68° F, and swim to find water of these temperatures. White Bass are related to Striped Bass and have lighter stripes on their sides. The biggest striped bass caught in North Carolina and the current state record is a massive 66-pound fish.

Spotted bass have rows of dark spots on their sides and an iridescent green pattern along their back. Spotted bass are also known as Kentucky's or redeye bass. They are a popular game fish, often mistaken for largemouth bass, but they have subtle differences like a a smaller mouth. They are known for their aggressive nature and tendency to school together. They also prefer rocky bottoms and being in deeper water compared to other bass who like shallow water. The biggest Spotted Bass caught in North Carolina weighed 6 lbs. 5 oz.

Smallmouth bass have a smaller mouth than the largemouth bass. They also have different markings and are lighter in color. They don't live in most lakes because they prefer living in colder water. They are typically found in the northern states in America because the water is cooler. The current world record smallmouth is an 11-pound, 15-ounce fish caught in Dale Hollow Lake. The biggest smallmouth bass in North Carolina weighed 10 pounds, 2 ounces.

The largemouth bass is the most sought-after bass in North America. Largemouth bass live in just about every lake in North America. They have great hearing and can hear a crayfish crawling on the bottom of the lake. The North Carolina state record for largemouth bass is 15 pounds, 14 ounces.

Sturgeons have sharp spines on their back, so be careful when handling them. Instead of scales, sturgeon skin is covered in bony plates called scutes, which can be very sharp on young sturgeon. Sturgeons have been around since the dinosaur days. Sturgeons mostly live in large, freshwater lakes and rivers. Their average lifespan is 50 to 60 years. They can grow to be quite large, with some reaching 6-8 feet long and weighing up to 300 pounds.

The walleye got its name because of its white looking eyes. Their eyes collect light, even in low light conditions. This means they can see in the dark. Because they can see in the dark, they mostly feed at night. During the daytime their eyes are very sensitive, so they usually head for deeper water or shady places. Walleye like to live in cooler water and are normally found in the upper part of North America. The biggest walleye caught in North Carolina weighed 13 pounds, 8 ounces.

Pickerel, also called pike, look like northern pike, but they are not. The Pike is larger in size than the Pickerel. The Pickerel has more spots than the Pike, but the Pike has spots on its fins and pickerel don't. The Pickerel has a dark bar beneath their eyes and northern pike don't. There are 2 types of Pickerel in North Carolina, Chain Pickerel, and Redfin Pickerel. The biggest pickerel ever caught in North Carolina was an 8-pound Chain Pickerel.

The muskellunge called the Musky or Muskie for short is one of the biggest game fish in freshwater lakes. They are hard to catch, they say it takes a thousand casts to catch one. They're stocked and sought by anglers in these connected cool-water river systems. Muskellunge (Muskie) are primarily found in the western mountain rivers like the New, Nolichucky, and French Broad Rivers, and reservoirs such as Fontana and Lake Adger and Hiwassee. The biggest muskellunge (muskie) recorded in North Carolina weighed 41 pounds, 8 ounces.

Brown trout can live up to 20 years. Brown exhibits a variety of colors and spotting patterns, with red spots surrounded by blue halos and black spots being common. Brown trout have higher tolerance for warmer waters than either the brook or rainbow trout. Brown trout can be found on almost every continent except Antarctica. The biggest brown trout ever caught in North Carolina weighed 24 pounds, 10 ounces.

Brook trout are characterized by their olive-green bodies with pale, worm-like markings, red spots with bluish halos, and orange-red fins with white and black edges. They can grow up to 12 inches in length. Brook trout are cold-water fish that prefer clean, clear, and cold streams, lakes, and ponds. The largest officially recognized Brook Trout in North Carolina weighed 7 pounds, 7 ounces.

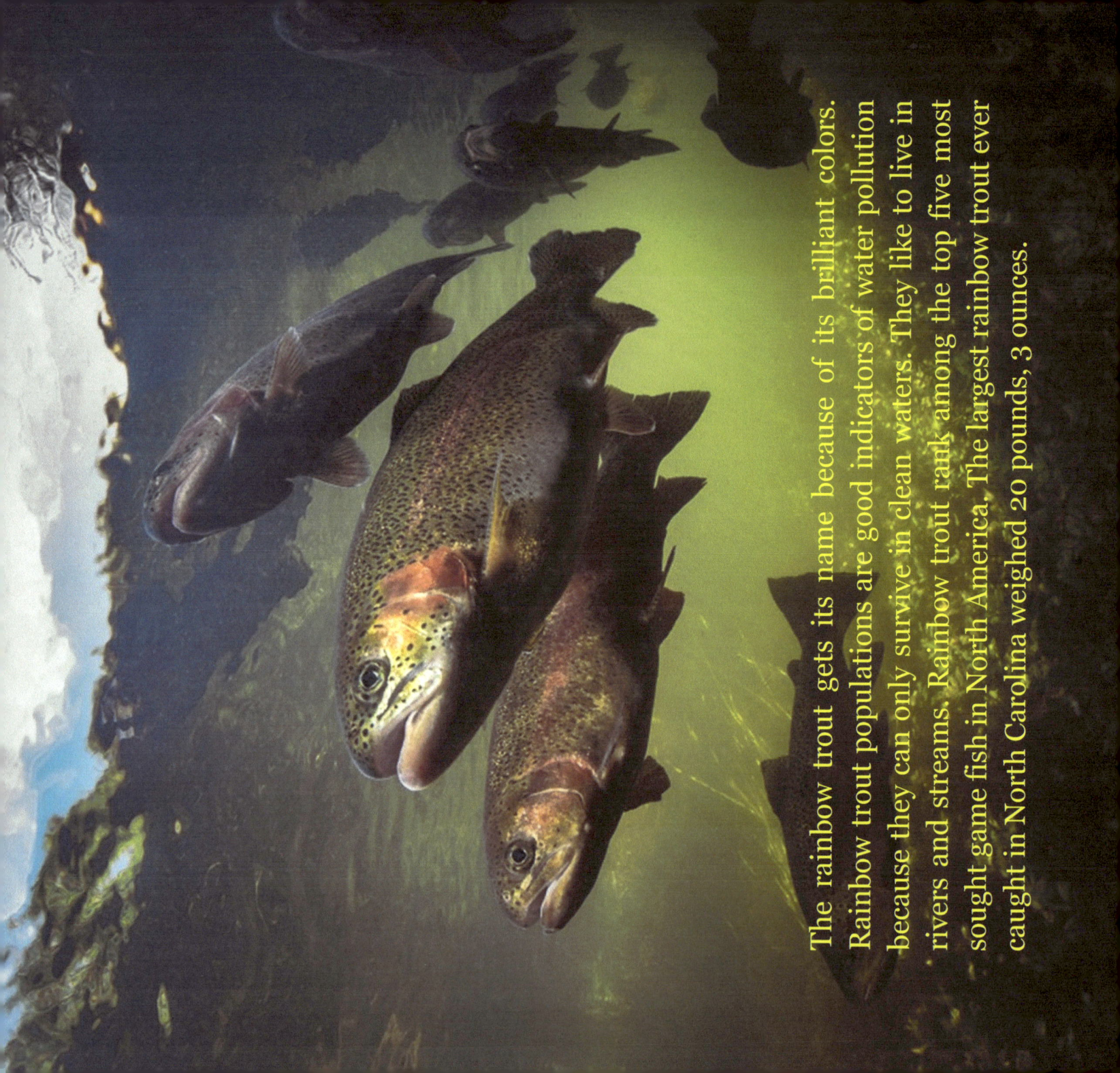

The rainbow trout gets its name because of its brilliant colors. Rainbow trout populations are good indicators of water pollution because they can only survive in clean waters. They like to live in rivers and streams. Rainbow trout rank among the top five most sought game fish in North America. The largest rainbow trout ever caught in North Carolina weighed 20 pounds, 3 ounces.

Interesting Fish Facts in North Carolina.

1 - North Carolina boasts over 250 freshwater fish species, including diverse bass (largemouth, smallmouth), sunfish, crappie, catfish, and native trout.

2 - The Brook Trout (specifically the Southern Appalachian Brook Trout) is North Carolina's official freshwater fish.

3 - Popular game fish include Largemouth Bass, Smallmouth Bass, and Black Crappie.

4 - The biggest freshwater fish caught in North Carolina is a Blue Catfish weighing 127 pounds, 1 ounce.

5 - The smallest freshwater fish caught in North Carolina is likely the Least Killifish.

6 - Bluegill, Crappie, Catfish, and Largemouth Bass are common in lakes and ponds.

7 - Major rivers hold various types of bass, catfish, and perch.

8 - Trout, Smallmouth Bass, and Rock Bass can be caught in the Blue Ridge and Appalachian Mountains.

Author Page

Billy Grinslott – Kinsey Marie Books

ISBN – 9781968228446

Thanks

www.ingramcontent.com/pod-product-compliance
Lightning Source LLC
Chambersburg PA
CBHW060849270326
41934CB00002B/61